Alexander Whyte, Teresa of Avila

Santa Teresa

An Appreciation

Alexander Whyte, Teresa of Avila

Santa Teresa
An Appreciation

ISBN/EAN: 9783741137990

Manufactured in Europe, USA, Canada, Australia, Japa

Cover: Foto ©Thomas Meinert / pixelio.de

Manufactured and distributed by brebook publishing software
(www.brebook.com)

Alexander Whyte, Teresa of Avila

Santa Teresa

Santa Teresa

an Appreciation

With some of the best passages
of the Saint's Writings Selected
Adapted and Arranged by

Alexander Whyte

D.D.

Oliphant Anderson & Ferrier

Saint Mary Street, Edinburgh, and

21 Paternoster Square, London

1897

Edinburgh : T. and A. CONSTABLE, Printers to Her Majesty

CONTENTS

APPRECIATION
AND INTRODUCTION

WITH a view to the work of my classes this session, I took old Abraham Woodhead's two black-letter quartos with me to the Engadine last July. And I spent every rainy morning and every tired evening of that memorable holiday month in the society of Santa Teresa and her excellent old-English translator. Till, ever, as I crossed the Morteratch and the Roseg, and climbed the hills around Maloggia and Pontresina, a voice would come after me, saying to me, Why should you not share all this spiritual profit and intellectual delight with your Sabbath evening congregations, and with your young men's and young women's classes ? Why should you not introduce Santa Teresa to her daughters in Edinburgh? For her daughters they are, so soon and as long as they live in self-knowledge and in self-denial, in humility and in meekness, and especially in unceasing prayer for themselves and for others.

A

And I am not without some assurance that in this present lecture I am both hearing and obeying one of those same locutions that Teresa heard so frequently, and obeyed with such instancy and fidelity and fruitfulness.

Luther was born in 1483, and he nailed his ninety-five theses to the door of the University Church of Wittenberg on the 31st October 1517. Loyola was born in 1491, and Xavier in 1506, and the Society of Jesus was established in 1534. Isabella the Catholic was born in 1451, and our own Protestant Elizabeth in 1533. The Spanish Inquisition began to sit in 1483, the Breviary was finally settled in 1568, and the Armada was destroyed in 1588. Columbus was born in 1446, and he set out on his great enterprise in 1492. Cervantes was born in 1547, and the First Part of his immortal work was published in 1605. And it is to be read in Santa Teresa's Breviary to this day that Teresa the Sinner was born on the 29th day of March 1515, at five o'clock in the morning. She died in 1582, and in 1622 she was publicly canonised at Rome along with Loyola and Xavier and two other Spanish saints.

Teresa was greatly blessed in both her

parents. 'It helped me much that I never saw my father or my mother respect anything in any one but goodness.' Her father was a great reader of the best books, and he took great pains that his children should form the same happy habit and should carefully cultivate the same excellent taste. Her mother, while a Christian gentlewoman of the first social standing, did not share her husband's love of serious literature. She passed far too much of her short lifetime among the romances of the day, till her daughter has to confess that she took no little harm from the books that did her mother no harm but pastime to read. As for other things, her father's house was a perfect model of the very best morals and the very best manners. Alonso de Cepeda was a well-born and a well-bred Spanish gentleman. He came of an ancient and an illustrious Castilian stock ; and, though not a rich man, his household enjoyed all the nobility of breeding and all the culture of mind and all the refinement of taste for which Spain was so famous in that great age. All her days, and in all her ups and downs in life, we continually trace back to Teresa's noble birth and noble upbringing no little of her supreme stateliness of deportment and serenity of manner

and chivalry of character. Teresa was a perfect
Spanish lady, as well as a mother in Israel, and
no one who ever conversed with her could for
a moment fail to observe that the oldest and
best blood of Spain mantled in her cheek and
shone in her eye. A lion encompassed by
crosses was one of the quarters of her father's
coat of arms. And Teresa took that up and
added out of it a new glory to all her father's
hereditary honours. For his daughter was all
her days a lioness palisaded round with crosses,
till by means of them she was transformed into
a lamb. But, all the time, the lioness was still
lurking there. Teresa's was one of those
sovereign souls that are born from time to
time as if to show us what our race was
created for at first, and for what it is still des-
tined. She was a queen among women. She
was in intellect the complete equal, and in still
better things than intellect far the superior,
of Isabella and Elizabeth themselves. As she
says in an outspoken autobiographic passage,
hers was one of those outstanding and tower-
ing souls on which a thousand eyes and tongues
are continually set without any one understanding them or comprehending them. Her
coming greatness of soul is foreseen by some
of her biographers in the attempt which she

made while yet a child to escape away into the country of the Moors in search of an early martyrdom, so that she might see her Saviour all the sooner, and stand in His presence all the purer. 'A woman,' says Crashaw, 'for angelical height of speculation: for masculine courage of performance, more than a woman; who, while yet a child, outran maturity, and durst plot a martyrdom.

> Scarce had she learnt to lisp the name
> Of martyr, yet she thinks it shame
> Life should so long sport with that breath,
> Which, spent, can buy so brave a death.
>
> Scarce had she blood enough to make
> A guilty sword blush for her sake ;
> Yet has she heart dares hope to prove
> How much less strong is death than love.
>
> Be love but there, let poor six years
> Be posed with the maturest fears
> Man trembles at, we straight shall find
> Love knows no nonage, nor the mind.'

Teresa's mother died just when her daughter was at that dangerous age in which a young girl needs a wise mother most ; 'the age when virtue should begin to grow,' as she says herself. Teresa was an extraordinarily handsome and attractive young lady, and the knowledge of that, as she tells us, made her very vain, and puffed up her heart with foolish imaginations.

She has a powerful chapter in the opening
of her Autobiography on dangerous com-
panionships in the days of youth. 'Oh that
all parents would take warning by me, and
would look carefully into their children's early
friendships!' She suffered terribly from bad
health all her days, and that severe chastise-
ment began to fall on her while she was yet a
beautiful girl. It was a succession of serious
illnesses, taken along with her father's scrupulous
care over her, that brought Teresa back to the
simple piety of her early childhood, and fixed
her for life in an extraordinary devotion to
God, and to all the things of God. When
such a change of heart and character comes to
a young woman among ourselves, she usually
seeks out some career of religion and charity
to which she can devote her life. She is found
labouring among the poor and the sick and the
children of the poor, or she goes abroad to
foreign mission work. In Teresa's land and
day a Religious House was the understood and
universal refuge for any young woman who
was in earnest about her duty to God and to
her own soul. In those Houses such young
women secluded themselves from all society
and gave themselves up to the care of the poor
and the young. In the more strict and enclosed

of those retreats the inmates never came out of doors at all, but wholly sequestered themselves up to a secret life of austerity and prayer. This was the ideal life led in those Houses for religious women. But Teresa soon found out the tremendous mistake she had made in leaving her father's family-fireside for a so-called Religious House. No sooner had she entered it than she was plunged headlong into those very same 'pestilent amusements,' the mere approach of which had made her flee to this supposed asylum. Though she is composing her Autobiography under the sharp eyes of her confessors, and while she is writing with a submissiveness and, indeed, a servility that is her only weakness, Teresa at the same time is bold enough and honest enough to tell us her own experiences of monastic life in language of startling strength and outspokenness. 'A short-cut to hell. If parents would take my advice, they would rather marry their daughters to the very poorest of men, or else keep them at home under their own eye. If young women will be wicked at home, their wickedness will not long be hidden at home; but in monasteries, such as I speak of, their worst wickedness can be completely covered up from every human eye. And all the time the poor things are not to blame. They only walk in the way that is shown them. Many of them are to be much pitied, for they honestly wish to withdraw from the world, only to find themselves in ten times worse worlds of sensuality and all other devilry. O my God! if I might I would fain speak of some of the occasions of sin from which Thou didst deliver me, and how I threw myself into them again. And of the risks I ran of utterly shipwrecking my character and good name and from which Thou didst rescue me. O Lord of my soul! how shall I be able to magnify Thy grace in those perilous years! At the very time that I was offending Thee most, Thou didst prepare me by a most profound compunction to taste of the sweetness of Thy recoveries and consolations. In truth, O my King, Thou didst administer to me the most spiritual and painful of chastisements : for Thou didst chastise my sins with great assurances of Thy love and of Thy great mercy. It makes me feel beside myself when I call to mind Thy great grace and my great ingratitude.'

This leads us up to the conception and commencement of that great work to which Teresa dedicated the whole of her after life,— the reformation and extension of the Religious

Houses of Spain. The root-and-branch reformation of Luther and his German and Swiss
colleagues had not laid much hold on Spain ;
and the little hold it had laid on her native land
had never reached to Teresa. Had Luther
and Teresa but met : had Melanchthon and
Teresa but met : had the best books of the
German and Swiss Reformation but come into
Teresa's hands : had she been somewhat less
submissive, and somewhat less obedient, and
somewhat less completely the slave of her
ecclesiastical superiors ; had she but once entered
into that intellectual and spiritual liberty wherewith Christ makes His people free,—what a
lasting blessing Teresa might have been made
to her native land ! But, as it was, Teresa's
reformation, while it was the salvation of
herself and of multitudes more who came under
it, yet as a monastic experiment and a church
movement, it ended in the strengthening and
the perpetuation of that detestable system of intellectual and spiritual tyranny which has been
the death of Spain from that day to this.
Teresa performed a splendid service inside the
Church to which she belonged: but that service
was wholly confined to the Religious Houses
that she founded and reformed. Teresa's
was intended to be a kind of counter-refor-

mation to the reformation of Luther and Melanchthon and Valdes and Valera. And such was the talent and the faith and the energy she brought to bear on the work she undertook, that, had it been better directed, it might have been blessed to preserve her beloved native land at the head of modern Christendom. But, while that was not to be, it is the immense talent, and the unceasing toil, and the splendid faith and self-surrender that Teresa brought to bear on her intramural reformation; and, all through that, on the working out of her own salvation,—it is all these things that go to make Teresa's long life so memorable and so impressive, not only in her own age and land and church, but wherever greatness of mind, and nobleness of heart, and sanctity of life, and stateliness of character are heard of and are esteemed.

Teresa's intellect, her sheer power of mind, is enough of itself to make her an intensely interesting study to all thinking men. No one can open her books without confessing the spell of her powerful understanding. Her books, before they were books, absolutely captivated and completely converted to her unpopular cause many of her most determined enemies. Again and again and again we find her con-

fessors and her censors admitting that both
her spiritual experiences and her reformation
work were utterly distasteful and very stum-
bling to them till they had read her own written
account, first of her life of prayer and then
of her reformation work. One after another
of such men, and some of them the highest
in learning and rank and godliness, on reading her autobiographic papers, came over to
be her fearless defenders and fast friends.
There is nothing more delightful in all her
delightful Autobiography, and in the fine
'censures' that have been preserved concerning it, than to read of the great and
learned theologians, the responsible church
leaders, and even the secret inquisitors who
came under the charm of her character and the
spell of her pen. 'She electrifies the will,'
confessed one of the best judges of good writing in her day. And old Bishop Palafox's
tribute to Teresa is far too beautiful to be
withheld. 'What I admire in her is the peace,
the sweetness, and the consolation with which
in her writings she draws us toward the best,
so that we find ourselves captured rather than
conquered, imprisoned rather than prisoners.
No one reads the saint's writings who does not
presently seek God, and no one through her

writings seeks God who does not remain in love with the saint. I have not met with a single spiritual man who does not become a passionate admirer of Santa Teresa. But her writings do not alone impart a rational, interior, and superior love, but a love at the same time practical, natural, and sensitive; and my own experience proves it to me that there exists no one who loves her but would, if the saint were still in this world, travel far to see and speak with her.' I wish much I could add to that Peter of Alcantara's marvellous analysis of Teresa's experiences and character. Under thirty-three heads that great saint sums up Teresa's character, and gives us a noble, because all unconscious, revelation of his own. And though Teresa has been dead for three hundred years, she speaks to this day in that same way: and that too in quarters in which we would little expect to hear her voice. In that intensely interesting novel of modern Parisian life, *En Route*, Teresa takes a chief part in the conversion and sanctification of the prodigal son whose return to his father's house is so powerfully depicted in that story. The deeply read and eloquent author of that remarkable book gives us some of the best estimates and descriptions of Santa Teresa that

I have anywhere met with. 'That cool-headed business woman . . . that admirable psychologist and of superhuman lucidity . . . that magnificent and over-awing saint . . . she has verified in her own case the supernatural experiences of the greatest mystics,—such are her unparalleled experiences in the supernatural domain. . . . Teresa goes deeper than any like writer into the unexplored regions of the soul. She is the geographer and hydrographer of the sinful soul. She has drawn the map of its poles, marked its latitudes of contemplation and prayer, and laid out all the interior seas and lands of the human heart. Other saints have been among those heights and depths and deserts before her, but no one has left us so methodical and so scientific a survey.' Were it for nothing else, the chapters on mystical literature in M. Huysmans' unfinished trilogy would make it a valued possession to every student of the soul of man under sin and under salvation. I await the completion of his Pilgrim's Progress with great impatience and with great expectation.

And then, absolutely possessed as Teresa always is by the most solemn subjects,— herself, her sin, her Saviour, her original method of prayer and her unshared experiences in prayer,—she showers upon us continually gleams and glances of the sunniest merriment, amid all her sighs and tears. She roasts in caustic the gross-minded, and the self-satisfied, and the self-righteous, as Socrates himself never roasted them better. Again, like his, her irony and her raillery and her satire are sometimes so delicate that it quite eludes you for the first two or three readings of the exquisite page. And then, when you turn the leaf, she is as ostentatiously stupid and ignorant and dependent on your superior mind as ever Socrates himself was. Till I shrewdly suspect that no little of that 'obedience' which so intoxicated and fascinated her inquisitors, and which to this day so exasperates some of her biographers, was largely economical and ironical. Her narrow cell is reported to have often resounded with peals of laughter to the scandal of some of her sisters. In support of all that, I have marked a score of Socratic passages in Woodhead, and Dalton, and Lewis, and Father Coleridge, and Mrs. Cunninghame Graham. They are very delicious passages and very tempting. But were they once begun there would be no end to them. You will believe Froude, for he is an admitted judge in all matters connected with the best literature, and he says

in his *Quarterly* article on Teresa's writings,
'The best satire of Cervantes is not more
dainty.'

The great work to which Teresa gave up
her whole life, after her full conversion, was
the purification of the existing monastic system,
and the multiplication and extension of Religious Houses of the strictest, severest, most
secluded, most prayerful, and most saintly life.
She had been told by those she too much
trusted, that the Church of Christ was being
torn in pieces in Germany, and in Switzerland,
and in France, and in England by a great out-
break of heretical error ; and, while the Society
of Jesus and the Secret Inquisition were established to cope with all such heresy, Teresa set
herself to counteract it by a widespread com-
bination of unceasing penance and intercessory
prayer.   It was a zeal without knowledge ;
but there can be no doubt about the sincerity,
the single-mindedness, and the strength of the
zeal.   For forty as hard-working years as ever
any woman spent in this world, Teresa laboured
according to her best light to preserve the
purity and the unity of the Church of Christ.
And the strength and the sagacity of mind,
the tact, the business talents, the tenacity of
will, the patience, the endurance, the perse-

verance, the sleepless watchfulness, and the abounding prayerfulness that she brought to bear on the reformation and multiplication of her fortresses of defence and attack in that holy war, all taken together, make up one of the most remarkable pages in the whole history of the Church of Christ. Her difficulties with Rome, with the Inquisition, with her more immediate superiors, confessors, and censors : and, most of all, with the ignorance, the stupidity, the laziness, the malice, and the lies of those monks and nuns whose reformation she was determined on : her endless journeys : her negotiations with church-leaders, land-owners, and tradesmen in selecting and securing sites, and in erecting new religious houses : the adventures, the accidents, the entertainments she met with : and the fine temper, the good humour, the fascinating character, the winning manners she everywhere exhibited ; and, withal, her incomparable faith in the Living God, and the exquisite inwardness, unconquerable assurance, and abounding fruitfulness of her own and unshared method and secret of prayer,—had Teresa not lived and died in Spain, and had she not spent her life and done her work under the Roman obedience, her name would have been a household word in Scotland.   As it is, she is not wholly unknown or unloved.   And as knowledge extends, and love, and good-will; and as suspicion, and fear, and retaliation, and party-spirit die out among us, the truth about Teresa and multitudes more will become established on clearer and deeper and broader founda-tions; and we shall be able to hail both her and multitudes more like her as our brothers and sisters in Christ, whom hitherto we have hated and despised because we did not know them, and had been poisoned against them.   I am a conspicuous case in point myself.   And when I have been con-quered by a little desultory reading and by a little effort after love no man need despair. And if you will listen to this lecture with a good and honest heart : with a heart that delights to hear all this good report about a fellow-believer : then He who has begun that good work in you will perfect it by books and by lectures like this, and far better than this, till you are taken absolutely captive to that charity which rejoiceth not in iniquity, but rejoiceth in the truth : and which beareth all things, believeth all things, hopeth all things, endureth all things.   Follow after charity, and begin with Santa Teresa.

Forbid it, mighty Love, let no fond hate
Of names or words so far prejudicate ;
Souls are not Spaniards too ; one friendly flood
Of baptism blends them all into one blood.
What soul soe'er in any language can
Speak heaven like hers, is my soul's countryman.

But the greatest and the best talent that God gives to any man or woman in this world is the talent of prayer. And the best usury that any man or woman brings back to God when He comes to reckon with them at the end of this world is a life of prayer. And those servants best put their Lord's money to the exchangers who rise early and sit late, as long as they are in this world, ever finding out and ever following after better and better methods of prayer, and ever forming more secret, more steadfast, and more spiritually fruitful habits of prayer : till they literally pray without ceasing, and till they continually strike out into new enterprises in prayer, and new achievements, and new enrichments. It was this that first drew me to Teresa. It was her singular originality in prayer and her complete captivity to prayer. It was the time she spent in prayer, and the refuge, and the peace, and the sanctification, and the power for carrying on hard and unrequited work that she all her life found in prayer. It was her fidelity and her

utter surrender of herself to this first and last
of all her religious duties, till it became more a
delight, and, indeed, more an indulgence, than
a duty.   With Teresa it was prayer first, and
prayer last, and prayer always.   With Teresa
literally all things were sanctified, and
sweetened, and made fruitful by prayer.   In
Teresa's writings prayer holds much the same
place that it holds in the best men and women
of Holy Scripture.   If I were to say that about
some of the ladies of the Scottish Covenant, you
would easily believe me.   But you must believe
me when I tell you that about a Spanish lady,
second to none of them in holiness of life, even
if her holy life is not all cast in our mould.   All
who have read the autobiographic *Apologia* will
remember the fine passage in which its author
tells us that ever since his conversion there have
been two, and only two, absolutely self-luminous
beings in the whole universe of being to him,—
God and his own soul.   Now, I do not remember that Newman even once speaks about
Teresa in any of his books, but I always think
of him and her together in this great respect.
GOD IS to them both, and to them both He is
a rewarder of them that diligently seek Him.
And it is just here, at the very commencement
and centre of divine things, that we all make

such shipwreck and come so short. The sense
of the reality of divine and unseen things in
Teresa's life of prayer is simply miraculous in a
woman still living among things seen and tem-
poral. Her faith is truly the substance of things
hoped for, and the evidence of things not seen.
Our Lord was as real, as present, as near, as
visible, and as affable to this extraordinary saint
as ever He was to Martha, or Mary, or Mary
Magdalene, or the woman of Samaria, or the
mother of Zebedee's children. She prepared
Him where to lay His head; she sat at His
feet and heard His word. She chose the better
part, and He acknowledged to herself and
to others that she had done so. She washed
His feet with her tears, and wiped them with
the hair of her head. She had been forgiven
much, and she loved much. He said to her,
Mary, and she answered Him, Rabboni. And
He gave her messages to deliver to His dis-
ciples, who had not waited for Him as she had
waited. Till she was able to say to them all
that she had seen the Lord, and that He had
spoken such and such things within her. And
hence arises what I may call the quite extraordinary purity and spirituality of her life of
prayer. ' Defecate ' is Goodwin's favourite
and constant word for the purest, the most

rapt, the most adoring, and the most spiritual prayer. 'I have known men'—it must have been himself—'who came to God for nothing else but just to come to Him, they so loved Him. - They scorned to soil Him and themselves with any other errand than just purely to be alone with Him in His presence. Friendship is best kept up, even among men, by frequent visits; and the more free and defecate those frequent visits are, and the less occasioned by business, or necessity, or custom they are, the more friendly and welcome they are.' Now, I have sometimes wondered what took Teresa so often, and kept her so long, alone with God. Till I remembered Goodwin's classical passages about defecated prayer, and understood something of what is involved and what is to be experienced in pure and immediate communion with God. And, then, from all that it surely follows, that no one is fit for one moment to have an adverse or a hostile mind, or to pass an adverse or a hostile judgment, on the divine manifestations that came to Teresa in her unparalleled life of prayer; no one who is not a man of like prayer himself; no, nor even then. I know all the explanations that have been put forward for Teresa's 'locutions' and revelations; but after anxiously weighing them all, the simplest explanation is also the most scientific, as it is the most scriptural. If our ascending Lord actually said what He is reported to have said about the way that He and His Father will always reward äll love to Him, and the keeping of all His commandments ; then, if there is anything true about Teresa at all, it is this, that from the day of her full conversion she lived with all her might that very life which has all these transcendent promises spoken and sealed to it. By her life of faith and prayer and personal holiness, Teresa made herself ' capable of God,' as one describes it, and God came to her and filled her with Himself to her utmost capacity, as He said He would. At the same time, much as I trust and honour and love Teresa, and much good as she has been made of God to me, she was still, at her best, but an imperfectly sanctified woman, and her rewards and experiences were correspondingly imperfect. But if a holy life before such manifestations were made to her, and a still holier life after them—if that is any test of the truth and reality of such transcendent and supernatural matters, —on her own humble and adoring testimony, and on the now extorted and now spontaneous testimony of absolutely all who lived near her, still more humility, meekness, lowly-minded-ness, heavenly-mindedness and prayerfulness demonstrably followed those inward and spiritual revelations to her of her Lord. In short and in sure, ye shall know them by their fruits. Do men gather grapes of thorns, or figs of thistles? On the whole, then, I for one am strongly disposed toward Teresa, even in the much-inculpated matter of her inward voices and visions. The wish may very possibly be father to the thought : but my thought leans to Teresa, even in her most astounding locutions and revelations; they answer so entirely to my read-ing of our Lord and of His words. I take sides, on the whole, with those theologians of her day, who began by doubting, but ended by believing in Teresa and by imitating her. They were led to rejoice that any contemporary and fellow-sinner had attained to such fellow-ship with God : and I am constrained to take sides with them. ' One day, in prayer, the sweetness was so great that I could not but contrast it with the place I deserved in hell. The sweetness and the light and the peace were so great that, compared with it, everything in this world is vanity and lies. I was filled with a new reverence for God. I saw His majesty and His power in a way I cannot describe, and the vision kept me in great tenderness and joy and humility. I cannot help making much of that which led me so near to God. I knew at that great moment what it is for a soul to be in the very presence of God Himself. What must be the condescension of His majesty seeing that in so short a time He left so great an impression and so great a blessing on my soul! O my Lord, consider who she is upon whom Thou art bestowing such unheard-of blessings! Dost Thou forget that my soul has been an abyss of sin? How is this, O Lord, how can it be that such great grace has come to the lot of one who has so ill deserved such things at Thy hands!' He who can read that, and a hundred passages as good as that, and who shall straightway set himself to sneer and scoff and disparage and find fault, he is well on the way to the sin against the Holy Ghost. At any rate, I would be if I did not revere and love and imitate such a saint of God. Given God and His Son and His Holy Spirit: given sin and salvation and prayer and ·a holy life; and, with many drawbacks, Teresa's was just the life of self-denial and repentance and prayer and communion with God that we should all live. It is not Teresa who is to be bemoaned and blamed and called bad names.

It is we who do all that to her who are beside
ourselves.   It is we who need the beam to be
taken out of our own eye.   Teresa was a
mystery and an offence; and, again, an en-
couragement and an example to the theologians
and the inquisitors of her day just as she still
is in our day.   She was a stumbling-stone, or
an ensample, according to the temper and disposition and character of her contemporaries,
and she is the same to-day.

The pressing question with me is not the
truth or the falsehood, the amount of reality or
the amount of imagination in Teresa's locutions and visions.   The pressing question with
me is this,—Why it is that I have nothing to
show to myself at all like them.   I think I could
die for the truth of my Lord's promise that
both He and His Father will manifest Themselves to those who love Him and keep His
words; but He never manifests Himself, to be
called manifestation, to me.   I am driven in
sheer desperation to believe such testimonies
and attainments as those of Teresa, if only to
support my failing faith in the words of my
Master.   I had rather believe every syllable of
Teresa's so-staggering locutions and visions than
be left to this, that ever since Paul and John went
home to heaven our Lord's greatest promises

have been so many idle words. It is open to
any man to scoff and sneer at Teresa's extraordinary life of prayer, and at the manifestations of the Father and the Son that were made
to her in her life of prayer, and some of her
biographers and censors among ourselves have
made good use of their opportunity. But I
cannot any longer sit with them in the seat of
the scorner, and I want you all to rise up and
leave that evil seat also. Lord, how wilt Thou
manifest Thyself in time to come to me? How
shall I attain to that faith and to that love and
to that obedience which shall secure to me the
long-withheld presence and indwelling of the
Father and the Son?

Teresa's *Autobiography*, properly speaking,
is not an autobiography at all, though it ranks
with *The Confessions*, and *The Commedia*, and
The Grace Abounding, and *The Reliquiae*, as one
of the very best of that great kind of book.
It is not really Teresa's *Life Written by Herself*,
though all that stands on its title-page. It is
only one part of her life: it is only her life of
prayer. The title of the book, she says in one
place, is not her life at all, but *The Mercies of
God*. Many other matters come up incidentally
in this delightful book, but the whole drift and

the real burden of the book is its author's life of prayer. Her attainments and her experiences in prayer so baffled and so put out all her confessors that, at their wits' end, they enjoined her to draw out in writing a complete account of a secret life, the occasional and partial discovery of which so amazed, and perplexed, and condemned them. And thus it is that we come to possess this unique and incomparable autobiography : this wonderful revelation of Teresa's soul in prayer. It is a book in which we see a woman of sovereign intellectual ability working out her own salvation in circumstances so different from our own that we have the greatest difficulty in believing that it was really salvation at all she was so working out. Till, as we read in humility and in love, we learn to separate-off all that is local, and secular, and ecclesiastical, and circumstantial, and then we immensely enjoy and take lasting profit out of all that which is so truly Catholic and so truly spiritual. Teresa was an extraordinary woman in every way : and that comes out on every page of her Autobiography. So extraordinary that I confess there is a great deal that she tells us about herself that I do not at all understand. She was Spanish, and we are Scottish. She and we are wide as the poles asunder. Her lot was cast of God in the sixteenth century, whereas our lot is cast in the nineteenth. She was a Roman Catholic mystic, and we are Evangelical Protestants. But it is one of the great rewards of studying such a life as Teresa's to be able to change places with her so as to understand her and love her. She was, without any doubt or contradiction, a great saint of God. And a great saint of God is more worthy of our study and admiration and imitation and love than any other study or admiration or imitation or love on the face of the earth. And the further away such a saint is from us the better she is for our study and admiration and imitation and love, if we only have the sense and the grace to see it.

Cervantes himself might have written Teresa's *Book of the Foundations*. Certainly he never wrote a better book. For myself I have read Teresa's *Foundations* twice at any rate for every once I have read Cervantes' masterpiece. For literature, for humour, for wit, for nature, for photographic pictures of the time and the people, her *Foundations* are a masterpiece also : and then, Teresa's pictures are pictures of the best people in Spain. And there was no finer people in the whole of Christendom in that day than the best of the Spanish people. God had much people in the Spain of that day, and he who is not glad to hear that will never have a place among them. The Spain of that century was full of family life of the most polished and refined kind. And, with all their declensions and corruptions, the Religious Houses of Spain enclosed multitudes of the most saintly men and women. 'I never read of a hermit,' said Dr. Johnson to Boswell in St. Andrews, 'but in imagination I kiss his feet : I never read of a monastery, but I could fall on my knees and kiss the pavement. I have thought of retiring myself, and have talked of it to a friend, but I find my vocation is rather in active life.' It was such monasteries as Teresa founded and ruled and wrote the history of that made such a sturdy Protestant as Dr. Johnson was say such a thing as that. *The Book of the Foundations* is Teresa's own account, written also under superior orders, of that great group of religious houses which she founded and administered for so many years. And the literature into which she puts all those years is literature of the first water. A thousand times I have been reminded of Don Quixote and Sancho Panza as I read Teresa's account of her journeys, and of the people, and of the escapades, and of the entertainments she met with. Yes, quite as good as Cervantes! yes, quite as good as Goldsmith!—I have caught myself exclaiming as I read and laughed till the tears ran down my cheeks. This is literature, this is art without the art, this is literary finish without the labour : and all laid out to the finest of all uses, to tell of the work of God, and of all the enterprises, providences, defeats, successes, recompenses, connected with it. The *Foundations* is a Christian classic even in Woodhead's and Dalton's and David Lewis's English, what must it then be to those to whom Teresa's exquisite Spanish is their mother-tongue!

If Vaughan had but read *The Foundations*, which he is honest enough to confess he had only glanced at in a French translation, it would surely have done something to make him reconsider the indecent and disgraceful attack which he makes on Teresa. His chapter on Teresa is a contemptuous and a malicious caricature. Vaughan has often been of great service to me, but if I had gone by that misleading chapter, I would have lost weeks of most intensely interesting and spiritually profitable reading. Vaughan's extravagant misrepresentation of Teresa will henceforth make me hesitate to receive his other judgments till I have read the books myself. I shall not tarry here to controvert Vaughan's utterly untruthful chapter on Teresa, I shall content myself with setting over against it Crashaw's exquisite *Hymn* and *Apology*, and especially his magnificent *Flaming Heart*.

Teresa's *Way of Perfection* is a truly fine book : full of freshness, suggestiveness, and power. So much so, that I question if William Law's *Christian Perfection* would ever have been written, but that Teresa had written on that same subject before him. I do not say that Law plagiarised from Teresa, but some of his very best passages are plainly inspired by his great predecessor. You will thank me for the following eloquent passage from Mrs. Cunninghame Graham, which so felicitously characterises this great book, and that in language such as I could not command. ' To my thinking Teresa is at her best in her *Way of Perfection* with its bursts of impassioned eloquence ; its shrewd and caustic irony ; its acute and penetrating knowledge of human character, the same in the convent as in the world ; above all in its sympathetic and tender instinct for the needs and difficulties of her daughters.   *The Perfection* represents the finished and magnificent fabric of the spiritual life.   Her words ring with a strange terseness and earnestness as she here pens her spiritual testament.   She points out the mischievous foibles, the little meannesses, the spirit of cantankerousness and strife, which long experience of the cloister had shown her were the besetting sins of the conventual life.   She places before them the loftier standard of the Cross.   Her words, direct and simple, ring out true and clear, producing somewhat the solemn effect of a Commination Service.'   Strong as that estimate is, *The Perfection* deserves every word of it and more.

Teresa thought that her *Mansions* was one of her two best books, but she was surely far wrong in that.   *The Mansions*, sometimes called *The Interior Castle*, to me at any rate, is a most shapeless, monotonous, and wearisome book. Teresa had a splendid imagination, but her imagination had not the architectonic and dramatic quality that is necessary for carrying out such a conception as that is which she has laid in the ground-plan of this book.   No one who has ever read *The Purgatorio* or *The Holy War* could have patience with the shapeless and inconsequent *Mansions*.   There is nothing that is new in the matter of the *Mansions*; there is nothing that is not found in a far better shape in some of her other books; and one is continually wearied out by her utter inability to handle the imagery which she will not let alone. At the same time, the persevering reader will come continually on characteristic things that are never to be forgotten as he climbs with Teresa from strength to strength on her way to her Father's House.

To my mind Teresa is at her very best, not in her *Mansions* which she made so much of, but in her *Letters* which she made nothing of. I think I prefer her *Letters* to all her other books. A great service was done to this fine field of literature when Teresa's letters were collected and published. What Augustine's editor has so well said about Augustine's letters I would borrow and would apply to Teresa's letters. All her other works receive fresh light from her letters. The subjects of her more elaborate writings are all handled in her letters in a far easier, a far more natural, and a far more attractive manner. It is in her letters that we first see the size and the strength and the sweep of her mind, and discover the deserved deference that is paid to her on all hands. Burdened churchmen, inquiring students in

c

the spiritual life, perplexed confessors, angry and remonstrating monks, husbands and wives, matrons and maidens, all find their way to Mother Teresa. Great bundles of letters are delivered at the door of her cell every day, and she works at her answers to those letters till a bird begins to flutter in the top of her head, after which her physician will not suffer her to write more than twelve letters at a downsitting. And what letters they are, all sealed with the name of JESUS—she will seal now with no other seal. What letters of a strong and sound mind go out under that seal! What a business head! What shrewdness, sagacity, insight, frankness, boldness, archness, raillery, downright fun! And all as full of splendid sense as an egg is full of meat. If Andrew Bonar had only read Spanish, and had edited Teresa's *Letters* as he has edited Rutherford's, we would have had that treasure in all our houses. As it is, Father Coleridge long ago fell on the happy idea of compiling a *Life of Teresa* out of her extant letters, and he has at last carried out his idea, if not in all its original fulness, yet in a very admirable and praiseworthy way. But I would like to know how many of the boasted literary and religious people of Edinburgh have bought and read

Father Coleridge's delightful book. A hundred? Ten? Five? I doubt it. Or how many have so much as borrowed from the circulating library Mrs. Cunninghame Graham's first-rate book? Of Teresa's *Letters*, that greatest living authority on Teresa says—' That long series of epistolary correspondence, so enchanting in the original. It is in her letters that Teresa is at her best. They reveal all her shrewdness about business and money matters ; her talent for administration ; her intense interest in life, and in all that is passing around her. Her letters show Teresa as the Castilian gentlewoman who not only treats on terms of perfect equality with people of the highest rank in the kingdom, but is in the greatest request by them. Her letters, of which probably only a tithe remains, show us how marvellously the horizon of her life had expanded, and how rapidly her fame had grown. Perhaps no more finished specimen of epistolary correspondence has ever been penned than those letters, written in the press of multifarious occupations, and often late at night when the rest of the convent was sleeping.'

Her confessor, who commanded Teresa to throw her *Commentary on the Song of Solomon* into the fire, was a sensible man and a true

friend to her reputation, and the nun who
snatched a few leaves out of the fire did
Teresa's fame no service. Judging of the
whole by the part preserved to us, there
must have been many things scattered up and
down the destroyed book well worthy of her
best pen. The 'instance of self-esteem' which
Teresa so delightfully narrates is well worth
all the burnt fingers its preservation had cost
the devoted sister: and up and down the
charred leaves there are passages on conduct
and character, on obedience and humility and
prayer, that Teresa alone could have written.
All the same, as a whole, her *Commentary on
the Song* is better in the fire.

Her *Seven Meditations on the Lord's Prayer*
ran no danger of the censor's fire. I have had
occasion to read all the best expositions of the
Lord's Prayer in our language, and I am
bound to say that for originality and striking
suggestiveness Teresa's *Seven Meditations* stands
alone. After I had written that extravagant
sentence I went back and read her little book
over again, so sure was I that I must have
overpraised it, and that I would not be
believed in what I have said concerning it.
But after another reading of the *Meditations*
I am emboldened to let the strong praise stand

in all its original strength. I have passages
marked in abundance to prove to demonstra-
tion the estimate I have formed of this beautiful
book, but I must forego myself the pleasure
and the pride of quoting them.

Sixteen Augustinian *Exclamations after having Communicated :* sixty-nine *Advices to Her
Daughters*, and a small collection of love-
enflamed *Hymns*, complete what remains to
us of Teresa's writings.

Teresa died of hard work and worry and
shameful neglect, almost to sheer starvation.
But she had meat to eat that all Anne
Bartholomew's remaining mites could not buy
for her dying mother. And, strong in the
strength of that spiritual meat, Teresa rose off
her deathbed to finish her work. She inspected
with all her wonted quickness of eye and love of
order the whole of the House into which she
had been carried to die. She saw everything put
into its proper place, and every one answering
to their proper order, after which she attended
the divine offices for the day, and then went
back to her bed and summoned her daughters
around her. 'My children,' she said, 'you
must pardon me much ; you must pardon me
most of all the bad example I have given you.
Do not imitate me. Do not live as I have

lived. I have been the greatest sinner in all the world. I have not kept the laws I made for others. I beseech you, my daughters, for the love of God, to keep the rules of your Holy Houses as I have never kept them. O my Lord,' she then turned to Him and said, 'the hour I have so much longed for has surely come at last. The time has surely come that we shall see one another. My Lord and Saviour, it is surely time for me to be taken out of this banishment and be for ever with Thee. The sacrifices of God are a broken spirit, a broken and a contrite heart, O God, Thou wilt not despise. Cast me not away from Thy presence, and take not Thy Holy Spirit away from me. Create in me a clean heart, O God.' 'A broken and a contrite heart; a broken and a contrite heart,' was her continual cry till she died with these words on her lips, 'A broken and a contrite heart Thou wilt not despise.' And, thus, with the most penitential of David's penitential Psalms in her mouth, and with the holy candle of her Church in her hand, Teresa of Jesus went forth from her banishment to meet her Bridegroom.

O sweet incendiary ! shew here thy art
Upon this carcass of a cold hard heart ;

Let all thy scatter'd shafts of light that play
Among the leaves of thy large books of day,
Combined against this breast at once break in
And take away from me myself and sin ;
This gracious robbery shall thy bounty be,
And thy best fortune such fair spoils of me.
O thou undaunted daughter of desires !
By all thy dower of lights and fires ;
By all the eagle in thee, all the dove ;
By all thy lives and deaths of love ;
By thy large draughts of intellectual day ;
And all thy thirsts of love more large than they ;
By all thy brim-filled bowls of fierce desire ;
By thy last morning's draught of liquid fire ;
By the full kingdom of that final kiss
That seized thy parting soul, and sealed thee His ;
By all the Heavens thou hast in Him,
(Fair sister of the Seraphim !) ;
By all of Him we have in thee ;—
Leave nothing of myself in me.
Let me so read thy life, that I
Unto all life of mine may die.

*** *The translations in the following pages are mainly those of Woodhead and Lewis.*

SOME SELECTED PASSAGES

I HAD a father and a mother who both feared God. My father had his chief delight in the reading of good books, and he did his best to give his children the same happy taste. This also helped me much, that I never saw my father or my mother regard anything but goodness. Though possessing very great beauty in her youth, my mother was never known to set any store by it. Her apparel, even in her early married life, was that of a woman no longer young. Her life was a life of suffering, her death was most Christian. After my mother's removal, I began to think too much about my dress and my· appearance, and I pursued many such like things that I was never properly warned against, full of mischief though they were both to myself and to others. I too early learned every evil from an immoral relative. I was very fond of this woman's company. I gossiped and talked with her continually. She assisted me to all the amusements I loved; and, what was worse, she found some very evil amusements for me, and in every way communicated to me her own vanities and mischiefs. I am amazed to think on the evil that

one bad companion can do ; nor could I have believed
it, unless I had known it by experience.   The
company and the conversation of this one woman so
changed me that scarcely any trace was left in me of
my natural disposition to virtue.   I became a perfect
reflection of her and of another who was as bad as
she was.

For my education and protection my father sent
me to the Augustinian Monastery, in which children
like myself were brought up.   There was a good
woman in that religious house, and I began gradually
to love her.   How impressively she used to speak to
me of God !   She was a woman of the greatest
good sense and sanctity.   She told me how she first
came to herself by the mere reading of these words
of the Gospel, 'Many are called and few chosen.'
This good companionship began to root out the bad
habits I had brought to that house with me ; but my
heart had by that time become so hard that I never
shed a tear, no, not though I read the whole Passion
through.   When at last I entered the Religious House
of the Incarnation for life, our Lord at once made me
understand how He helps those who do any violence to
themselves in order to serve Him.   No one observed
this violence in me.   They saw nothing in me but
the greatest goodwill.   At that sore step I was filled
with a joy so great that it has never wholly left me to
this day.   God converted the dryness of my soul into
the greatest tenderness, immediately on my taking
up that cross.   Everything in religion was now a
real delight to me.   I had more pleasure now in
sweeping the house than I had in all the balls and

dances I had forsaken for His sake. Whenever I remember those early days, it makes me ready to take up any cross whatsoever. For I know now by a long and a various experience that His Majesty richly rewards even in this life all the self-denial that we do for His sake and service. I know this by many experiences; and if I were a person who had to advise and guide God's people, I would urge them to fear no difficulty whatsoever in the path of duty : for our God is omnipotent, and He is on our side. May He be blessed for ever ! Amen.

O my supreme Good and my true Rest, I know not how to go on when I call those happy days to mind, and think of all my evil life since then ! My tears ought to be tears of blood. My heart ought to break. But Thou, Lord, hast borne with me for almost twenty years, till I have had time to improve. And all that it might be better known to me who Thou art and what I am. Woe is me, my Maker ! I have no excuse, I have only blame. Let Thy mercy, O Lord, rest on me. Other women there have been who have done great deeds in Thy service, but I am good only to talk : all my goodness ends in so many words : that is all my service of Thee, my God. Cost me what it may, let me not go on coming to Thee with idle words and empty hands, seeing that the reward of every one will be according to his works. Depart not from me, and I can do all things. Depart from me, and I shall return to whence I was taken, even to hell.

One of the reasons that move me, who am what I am, to write all this even under obedience, and to

give an account of my wretched life, and of the graces
the Lord hath wrought in me is this,—and would
that I were a person of authority, and then people
would perhaps believe what I say. This then is
what I would say and repeat continually if any one
would hear me. Let no one ever say: If I fall into
sin, I cannot then pray. In this the devil turned
his most dreadful batteries against me. He said to
me that it showed very little shame in me if I could
have the face to pray, who had just been so wicked.
And under that snare of Satan I actually as good as
gave up all prayer for a year and a half. This was
nothing else but to throw myself straight down into
hell. O my God, was there ever such madness as
mine! Where could I think to find either pardon for
the past, or power for the time to come, but from
Thee? What folly to the stumbler to run away
from the light! Let all those who would give
themselves to prayer, and to a holy life, look well
to this. They should know that when I was shun-
ning prayer because I was so bad, my badness became
more abandoned than ever it had been before. Rely
on the waiting and abounding goodness of God,
which is infinitely greater than all the evil you can
do. When we acknowledge our vileness, He re-
members it no more. I grew weary of sinning
before God grew weary of forgiving my sin. He
is never weary of giving grace, nor are his com-
passions to be exhausted. May He be blessed for
ever, amen: and may all created things praise Him!

I have made a vow—[it is known as ‘the Teresian
vow,’ ‘the seraphic vow,’ ‘the most arduous of vows,’

'a vow yet unexampled in the Church'], a vow never to offend God in the very least matter. I have vowed that I would rather die a thousand deaths than do anything of that kind, knowing I was doing it. I am resolved also, never to leave anything whatsoever undone that I consider to be still more perfect, and more for the honour of our Lord. Cost me what pain it may, I would not leave such an act undone for all the treasures of the world. If I were to do so, I do not think I could have the face to ask anything of God in prayer : and yet, for all that, I have many faults and imperfections remaining in me to this day.

ON THE GODHEAD

On one occasion when I was in prayer I had a vision in which I saw how all things are seen in God. I cannot explain what I saw, but what I saw remains to this day deeply imprinted on my soul. It was a great act of grace in God to give me that vision. It puts me to unspeakable confusion, shame, and horror whenever I recall that magnificent sight, and then think of my sin. I believe that had the Lord been pleased to send me that great revelation of Himself earlier in my life, it would have kept me back from much sin. The vision was so delicate, so subtle, and so spiritual, that my hard understanding cannot, at this distance of time, close with it ; but, to make use of an illustration, it was something like this. Suppose the Godhead to be a vast globe of light, a globe larger than the whole world, and that all our actions are seen in that all-embracing globe. It was something like that I saw. For I saw all my most filthy actions gathered up and reflected back upon me from that World of light. I tell you it was a piteous and a dreadful thing to see. I knew not where to hide myself, for that shining light, in which was no darkness at all, held the whole world within it, and all worlds. You will see that I could not flee from its presence. Oh that they could be made to see this who commit deeds of darkness! Oh that they but saw that there is no place secret from God : but that all they do is done before Him, and in Him ! Oh the madness of committing sin in the immediate presence of a Majesty so great, and to whose holiness all our sin is so hateful. In this also I saw His great mercifulness in that He suffers such a sinner as I am still to live.

ON THE SOUL

O my God, what unspeakable sufferings our souls have to endure because they have lost their liberty, and are not their own masters! What tortures come on them through that ! I sometimes wonder how I can live through such agony of soul as I myself suffer. God be praised who gives me His own life in my soul, so that I may escape from so deadly a death ! My soul has indeed received great strength from His Divine Majesty. He has had compassion on my great misery, and has helped me. Oh, what a distress it is for my soul to have to return to hold commerce with this world after having had its conversation in heaven ! To have to play a part in the sad farce of this earthly life ! And yet I am in a strait betwixt two. I cannot run away from this world. I must remain in it till my discharge comes. But, meantime, how keen is my captivity; how wretched in my own soul am I. And one of my worst distresses is this, that I am alone in my exile. All around me people seem to have found their aim and end in life in this horrible prison-house, and to have said, Soul, take thine ease. But the life of my soul is a life of incessant trouble. The cross is always on my shoulder; at the same time I surely make some progress. God is the Soul of my soul. He engulfs into Himself my soul. He enlightens and strengthens my soul. He attends to my soul night and day. He gives my soul more and more grace. This has not come about of myself. No effort of mine brought this about. His Majesty does it all. And He has held me by the hand, that I might not go back. For this reason, it seems to me, the soul in which God works His grace, if it walks in humility and in fear, it may be led into whatsoever temptation, and thrown into whatsoever company, and it will only gain new strength there, and win new victories and spoils there. Those are strong souls which are chosen of the Lord to work for the souls of others. At the same time, their best strength is not their own. All that such souls ever attain to and perform, all these things only make them more humble, and therefore more strong; more able to despise the things of this world, and to lay up their treasure in those things which God hath prepared for them that love Him. May it please His Majesty that the great munificence with which He has dealt with my soul, miserable sinner that I am, may have some weight with some of those who read this, so that they may be strong and courageous to give up everything at once and most willingly for such a God !

ON GOD IN THE SOUL

This has done me a great deal of good, and it has affected me much and opened my eyes in many ways. It is an ennobling thing to think that God is more in the soul of man than He is in aught else outside of Himself. They are happy people who have once got a hold of this glorious truth. In particular, the Blessed Augustine testifies that neither in the house, nor in the church, nor anywhere else, did he find God, till once he had found Him in himself. Nor had he need to go up to heaven, but only down into himself to find God. Nay, he took God to heaven with him when at last he went there.

Now consider what our Master teaches us to say : 'Our Father which art in heaven.' Think you it concerns you little to know where and what that heaven is, and where your Heavenly Father is to be sought and found ? I tell you that for vagrant minds it matters much not only to believe aright about heaven, but to procure to understand this matter by experience. It is one of those things that strongly bind the understanding and recollect the soul. You already

know that God is in all places : in fine, that where
God is there heaven is, and where His Majesty
most reveals Himself there glory is.   Consider again
what Saint Augustine said, that he sought God in
many places, till at last he came to find Him within
himself.   You need not go to heaven to see God,
or to regale yourself with God.   Nor need you
speak loud as if He were far away.   Nor need you
cry for wings like a dove so as to fly to Him.   Settle
yourself in solitude, and you will come upon God in
yourself.   And then entreat Him as your Father,
and relate to Him your troubles.   Those who can
in this manner shut themselves up in the little
heaven of their own hearts, where He dwells who
made heaven and earth, let them be sure that they
walk in the most excellent way : they lay their pipe
right up to the fountain.   To keep the eyes shut
is an excellent practice in prayer, because it is a
summons and an assistance to turn the eyes of the
soul within, where God dwells and waits in Christ
to be gracious.   Account thus, that there is a great
and beautiful palace in your soul ; that its structure
is all of gold and precious stones ; that your gifts
and graces are those shining stones, and that the
greater your virtues are the more those precious
stones sparkle.   And, also, that in this palace the Great
King is your guest.   He sits on the innermost seat
of your heart, and holds it to be His best and bravest
throne.   This will seem to some a silly fiction.   And
yet, if you will believe it, fiction as it is, it will help
you much ; you especially who are women.   For
we women sorely want such assistance to our

D

thoughts. And, God grant that it be only women who need such assistance to show them how base is the use they make of themselves. There should be some difference between us, both men and women, and the brute beasts. The brute beasts are nowhere said to be temples of God, and they are nowhere called to account because their god is their belly. O great God, I tremble to see that I have written such a page as the above, being such a wretch as I am. My daughters, in their own goodness, will be tempted to think that all this is true of myself, and that is a terrible thought to me. On the other hand, it is true of God and their own souls. Now let men pass a thousand censures on me, and on my way of teaching the truth. What of that, if only God and His ways be a little better known and loved ! My sisters, the King is in His palace all this time. There are hostile invasions of His borders, and inroads made into His territories, but He abides all the time on His throne. I smile at the weakness and unworthiness of all those comparisons of palaces, and thrones, and shining stones, and enemies on the border. They in no way satisfy me. But I am a woman, and I can find out no better words for you women. Think and say of my words what you please. The thing that I have spoken to you is the truth.

ON THE LOVE OF GOD

The true proficiency of the soul consists not so much in deep thinking or eloquent speaking or beautiful writing as in much and warm loving.

Now if you ask me in what way this much and warm love may be acquired, I answer,—By resolving to do the will of God, and by watching to do His will as often as occasion offers. Those who truly love God love all good wherever they find it. They seek all good to all men. They encourage all good in all men. They commend all good, they always unite themselves with all good, they always acknowledge and defend all good. They have no quarrels. They bear no envy. O Lord, give me more and more of this blessed love. Grant me grace not to quit this underworld life till I no longer desire anything, nor am capable of loving anything, save Thee alone. Grant that I may use this word 'love' with regard to Thee alone, since there is no solidity for my love to rest on save in Thee. The soul has her own ways of understanding, and of finding in herself, by certain signs and great conjectures, whether she really loves His Divine Majesty or no. Her love is full of high impulses, and longings to see and to be with and to be like God. All else tires and wearies out the soul. The best of created things disappoint and torment the soul. God alone satisfies the soul, till it is impossible to dissemble or mistake such a love. When once I came to see the great beauty of our Lord, it turned all other comeliness to corruption to me. My heart could rest on nothing and on no one but Himself. When anything else would enter my heart I had only to turn my eyes for a moment in upon that Supreme Beauty that was engraven within me. So that

it is now impossible that any created thing can
so possess my soul as not to be instantly expelled,
and my mind and heart set free by a little effort to
recover the remembrance of the goodness and the
beauty of our Lord. Good God! What a difference
there is between the love of the Creator and the love
of the creature! May His Divine Majesty vouchsafe
to let us see and taste and understand something of
this before He takes us out of this prison-house life,
for it will be a magnificent comfort in the hour of
death to know that we are on our way to be judged
by Him whom we have loved above all things.
We are not going to a strange country, since it is
His country whom we love and who loves us.
These things being so, I have this very day solaced
my soul with our Lord, and have made my moan to
Him in this manner. O my Lord, why keepest
Thou Thy servant in this miserable life so long,
where all is such vexation, and disappointment, and
manifold trouble? And not only keepest me so
long in this banishment, but so hidest Thyself from
me. Is this worthy of Thee and of Thy great
goodness? Were I what Thou art, and wert Thou
what I am, Thou wouldest not have to endure it at
my hands. I beseech Thee, O my Lord, to consider that this is a kind of injury and wrong to
proceed after this manner with one who loves Thee
so much. This and the like have come into my
heart to say: though my bed in hell better becomes
me than so to speak to my Lord. At the same time,
the love I bear my Lord sometimes so consumes me
that I am beside myself, till I scarce know what I

say or do; and then I find myself making such unbecoming complaints that I am amazed our Lord endures them at my hands. Eternal praise to so good a Lord!

ON THE LOVE OF OUR NEIGHBOUR

There are only two duties that our Lord requires of us,—the love of God, and the love of our neighbour. And, in my opinion, the surest sign for discovering our love to God is our love to our neighbour. And be assured that the further you advance in the love of your neighbour, the further you are advancing in the love of God likewise. But, oh me, how many worms lie gnawing at the roots of our love to our neighbour! Self-love, self-esteem, fault-finding, envy, anger, impatience, scorn. I assure you I write this with great grief, seeing myself to be so miserable a sinner against all my neighbours. Our Lord, my sisters, expects works. Therefore when you see any one sick, compassionate her as if she were yourself. Pity her. Fast that she may eat. Wake that she may sleep. Again, when you hear any one commended and praised, rejoice in it as much as if you were commended and praised yourself. Which, indeed, should be easy, because where humility truly is, praise is a torment. Cover also your sister's defects as you would have your own defects and faults covered and not exposed. As often as occasion offers, lift off your neighbour's burden. Take it off her heart and on upon yourself. Satan himself would not be Satan any longer if he could once love his neighbour as himself.

Endeavour, my daughters, all you can, to be affable to all. Demean yourselves so that all who have to do with you may love your conversation, so as to desire after your way of life. Let no one be affrighted or turned away from the life of virtue and religion by your gloom and morosity. This concerns religious women very much. The more holy they are, the more affable and sociable should they study to be. Never hold aloof from others because their conversation is not altogether to your taste. Love them, and they will love you, and then they will converse with you, and will become like you, and better than you. Let not your soul coop itself up in a corner. For, instead of attaining to greater sanctity in a proud, and disdainful, and impatient seclusion, the devil will keep you company there, and will do your sequestered soul much mischief. Bury evil affections in good works. Wherefore be accessible and affable to all, and all in love. Love is an endless enchantment, and spell, and fascination.

ON OUR SINFULNESS

This is a very fit place for thinking on our wounds, and bruises, and putrifying sores: the blindness of our minds, the depravity and the bondage of our wills, the forgetfulness of our memories, the slipperiness of our tongues, the levity and frivolity of our hearts, with all their extravagances, presumptions, neglects. In fine, let there be no spiritual wound within us, great or small, old or new, which we do not daily discover and lay open to our Sovereign Physician, beseeching of Him a remedy. This day it is very proper to call to mind the five fountains of our Lord's wounds, which are still open, and will remain open till the last day for the cure of all the sores of our souls. And since out of His wounds we receive our spiritual health, let us mollify our wounds with the ointment of mortification and humility and meekness: in all things always employing ourselves for the benefit of our neighbour. Since, though we cannot have our Lord visibly and in presence beside us, we have our neighbour, who for the ends of love and loving service is as good as our Lord Himself.

ON THE WORLD

I saw that rich and great as she was, she was still a woman, and as much liable to all manner of passion and all womanly weakness as I was myself. I saw as I lived in her house that rank is of little worth, and the higher it is, the greater the trouble and the anxiety it brings with it. Great people must be careful of their dignity. It will not suffer them to live at ease. They must eat at fixed hours and by rule, for everything must be according to their state, and not according to their constitutions. And they have frequently to take food more fitted for their state than for their liking. So it was that I came to hate the wish to be a great lady. God deliver me from this artificial and evil life! Then, as to servants, though this lady has very good servants, how slight is the trust she is able to put in them. One must not be conversed with more than the rest, otherwise he is envied and hated of all the rest. This of itself is a slavery; and it is another of the lies of the world to call such people masters and mistresses, who, in reality, are nothing but slaves in a thousand ways. I really see nothing good in the world and its ways but this, that it will not tolerate the smallest fault in those who are not its own. For by detracting, and fault-finding, and evil-reporting on the good, the world greatly helps to perfect them. He who will not die to the world shall die by it. O wretched world! Bless God, my daughters, that He has chosen and enabled you to turn your backs for ever on a thing so base. The world is to be known by this also, that it esteems a man not by what he is, but by what he possesses : by what is in his purse : and, that failing, the honour and esteem of the world instantly fail also. O our Lord; Supreme Power, Supreme Goodness, Supreme Truth ; Thy perfections are without beginning and without end. They are infinite and incomprehensible. They are a bottomless ocean of beauty. O my God, that I had the eloquence of an angel's speech to set forth Thy goodness and Thy truth, and to win all men over to Thee !

ON EVIL-SPEAKING

After my vow of perfection I spake not ill of any creature, how little soever it might be. I scrupulously avoided all approaches to detraction. I had this rule ever present with me, that I was not to wish, nor assent to, nor say such things of any person whatsoever, that I would not have them say of me. And as time went on, I succeeded in persuading those who were about me to adopt the same habit, till it came to be understood that where I was absent persons were safe. So they were also with all those whom I so instructed. Still, for all that, I have a sufficiently strict account to give to God for the bad example I am to all about me in some other respects. May it please His Majesty to forgive me, for I have been the cause of much evil. For one thing, the devil sometimes fills me with such a harsh and cruel temper : such a spirit of anger and hostility at some people, that I could eat them up and annihilate them. At the same time, concerning things said of myself in detraction, and they are many, and are very prejudicial to me, I find myself much improved. These things make little impression upon me. I am under them as a deaf man that hears not, and as a man in whose mouth there is no retaliation. Nay, I almost always see that my greatest detractors have only too good reason for what they say. In this way my soul actually gains peace and strength under detraction, till it becomes a great favour done me, and a great advantage. Upon betaking myself to prayer, I find in my heart neither repugnance at my detractors nor enmity. For, although, when I first hear the detraction, it causes me a little disconcert, yet not any long-lasting disquiet or alteration. Nay, sometimes when I see people take pity on me because of my detractors, I laugh at them, so little do all my detractors now hurt me.

ON SELF-EXCUSING

That which I am now to persuade you to, namely, the not excusing of yourselves, causes a great confusion in me. For it is a very perfect quality and of great merit; and I ought far better to practise what I tell you concerning this excellent virtue. I confess myself to be but little improved in this noble duty. For it is a mark of the deepest and truest humility to see ourselves condemned without cause, and to be silent under it. It is a very noble imitation of our Lord. Were I truly humble, I would desire disesteem, even though having in the matter in hand given no real offence. Here no bodily strength is needed, my daughters, nor any one's assistance, but God's. How well is this written, and how ill is it practised by the writer! Indeed, I never could make trial of this grace in any matter of consequence, because I never heard of any one speaking ill of me, but I immediately saw how far short he came of the full truth. For, if he was wrong or exaggerated in his particulars, I had offended God much more in other matters that my detractor knew nothing about. And, methought, God favoured me much in not proclaiming my secret sins to all men. And, thus, I am very glad that my detractor should ever report a trifling lie about me, rather than the terrible truth.

O my Lord, when I remember in how many ways Thou didst suffer detraction and misrepresentation, who in no way deserved it, I know not where my senses are when I am in such a haste to defend and

excuse myself. Is it possible that I should desire any
one to speak any good of me, or to think it, when so
many ill things were thought and spoken of Thee !
What is this, O Lord ; what do we imagine to get
by pleasing worms, or being praised by them ? What
about being blamed by all men, if only we stand at
last blameless before Thee !

ON PRAISE, PRECEDENCY, AND POINTS
OF HONOUR

Observe carefully the stirrings of your heart in
matters of superiority. Pray to be delivered from
such thoughts as these : I am older. I deserve
better. I have laboured more. I have more talent.
Such thoughts are the plague and poison of the
heart. Believe me, if there remain in you any
allowed hankerings after the praises of men, though
you may have spent many years in prayer, or rather
in idle forms of prayer, you have made no progress,
and never will, till your heart is crucified to the
approval and the praise of men. If you feel in yourself any point of honour, any pride, any desire of
eminence or pre-eminence, you must free yourself
from that abominable bondage, and for that chain
there is no hammer and file like humility and prayer.
Among the rest of my great imperfections this was
one. I had very little knowledge of my Breviary, or
of that which was to be sung in the choir, and all
the while I saw that some other novices could in-
struct me. But I was too proud to ask any questions.
I was afraid that my great ignorance should be discovered. Shortly afterwards a good example was set

before me, and then, when God had once opened my
eyes to my sinful pride, I was content to ask informa-
tion and the help even of little children.   And yet,—
and this surprised me, I lost no credit or honour
thereby.   Nay, it seemed to me that my Lord
after that gave me better skill and a better
memory.   I could sing but very ill, and I was
troubled at this, not because I failed in my worship
of God, but because so many heard me, and thus I
was disturbed on the mere point of honour and
praise.   I told them that I could not do what others
did, and what was expected of me.   At first I
had some difficulty in this, but it soon became
both natural and pleasant to me to tell the truth.
By these nothings,—and they are really nothings, and
I am sufficiently nothing when such things could
put me to so much pain,—and by little and little
His Divine Majesty vouchsafed to supply me with
strength.   I was never good at the choir, but I tried
to do my part for it in folding up the mantles of the
singers ; and, methought, in that I was serving the
angels of God who so well praised Him.   I did that
also by stealth, such was my pride, and my pride was
hurt when they discovered what I did.   O my Lord,
who that ever reads this can fail to despise and abhor
me ?   I beseech Thy Divine Majesty that I may soon
be able to leave all such vanities as the praise and
blame of men, and seek Thy praise only !   And then
add this, which is worth knowing.   The devil will
not dare to tempt one to pride or precedency who is
truly humble ; because, being very crafty, he fears
defeat.   If you are truly humble, you will only grow

in that grace by every temptation to pride or praise. For, immediately on the temptation, you will reflect on your whole past life and present character, and on the stupendous humility of Jesus Christ. And by these considerations your tempted soul will come off so victorious, that the enemy will think twice before he comes back, for fear of a broken head.

ON HUMILITY

Keep yourselves, my daughters, from that false humility which the devil suggests concerning the greatness of your sins. For hereby he is wont to disquiet our souls after sundry sorts, and to draw us off Holy Communion, and also from prayer. It is sometimes a great and a true humility to esteem ourselves as bad as may be, but at other times it is a false and a spurious humility. I know it, for I have experienced it. True humility, however great, does not disquiet nor disorder the soul. It comes with great peace, and great serenity, and great delight. Though we should see our utter wickedness, and how truly we deserve to be in hell, and think that both God and man must despise and abhor us; yet, if this be a true humility, it comes with a certain sweetness and satisfaction attending it. This humility does not stifle nor crush the soul. It rather dilates the soul, and disposes the soul for the better service of God. While that other sorrow troubles all, and confounds all, and destroys all. It is the devil's humility when he gets us to distrust God. When you find yourselves thus, lay aside all thinking on your own misery, and meditate on the infinite mercy of God, and on the inexhaustible merit and grace of Jesus Christ.

I was once considering what the reason was why our Lord loved humility in us so much, when I suddenly remembered that He is essentially the Supreme Truth, and that humility is just our walking in the truth. For it is a very great truth that we have no good in us, but only misery and nothingness, and he who does not understand this walks in lies: but he who understands this the best is the most pleasing to the Supreme Truth. May God grant us this favour, sisters, never to be without the humbling knowledge of ourselves.

O Sovereign Virtues! O Ladies of all the creatures! O Empresses of the whole world! Whoever hath you may go forth and fight boldly with all hell at once. Let your soldiers not fear, for victory is already theirs. They only fear to displease God. They constantly beseech Him to maintain all the virtues in them. It is true these virtues have this property, to hide themselves from him who possesses them, so that he never sees them in himself, nor thinks that he can ever possess a single one of them. Other men see all the virtues in him, but he so values them that he still pursues them, and seeks them as something never to be attained by such as he is. And Humility is one of them, and is Queen and Empress and Sovereign over them all. In fine, one act of true humility in the sight of God is of more worth than all the knowledge, sacred and profane, in the whole world.

ON SORROW FOR SIN

It is indeed a very great misery to live on in this evil world where our enemies are ever at our gate, and where we can neither eat nor sleep in peace, but are compelled to have our armour on night and day. There is no rest here, nor happiness, nor will be till we are with the Everlastingly Blessed. As I write I am seized with terror, lest I should never escape this sinful life. Pray for me, my daughters, that Christ may ever live in me: for, otherwise, what security can there be for such as I am, who have been so wicked. You may sometimes have thought, my daughters, that those to whom the Lord particularly communicates Himself, will · be henceforth secure of enjoying Him for ever, and that they will have no need to fear or bewail their former sins. But this is a great mistake. Sorrow for sin increases in proportion as more and more grace is received from God. And I, for my part, believe, that this bitter sorrow will never leave us till we come where neither sin nor anything else will ever disquiet us. True, both past sin, and present sinfulness, affect us more at one time than at another; and, likewise, in a different manner. I know one who often wishes for death, that she may be freed from the torment of her sinful heart. No one's sins can equal hers, because there can be no one who has obtained such favours of her God. Her fear is not so much of hell, as that she should so grieve God's Holy Spirit, that He will be wearied out, and will forsake her, and leave her in her sins. This fear and pain is not at all eased by believing that her past sins have all been forgiven and forgotten of God. Nay, her fear and pain but increase by seeing such mercy extended toward a woman who deserves nothing but hell.

ON LEARNING AND INTELLECT

I always had a great respect and affection for intellectual and learned men. It is my experience that all who intend to be true Christians will do well to treat with men of mind and books about their souls. The more learning our preachers and pastors have the better. For if they have not much experience themselves, yet they know the Scriptures and the recorded experiences of the saints better than we do. The devil is exceedingly afraid of learning, especially where it is accompanied with humility and virtue. For my own part, I bless God continually, and we women, and all such as are not ourselves intellectual or learned, are always to give God infinite thanks that there are some men in the world who take such great pains to attain to that knowledge which we need but do not possess. And it delights me to see men taking the immense trouble they do take to bring me so much profit, and that without any trouble to me. I have only to sit still and hear them. I have only to come and ask them a question. Let us pray for our teachers, for what would we do without them. I beseech the Lord to bless our teachers, that they may be more and more a blessing to us.

When I spoke of humility, it must not be understood as if I spoke against aspiring after the highest
things that mind and heart and life can attain to.
For though I have no ability for the wisdom and the
knowledge of God myself, and am so miserable that
God did me a great favour in teaching me the very
lowliest truths : yet, in my judgment, learning and
knowledge are very great possessions, and a great
assistance in the life of prayer, if only they are always
accompanied with humility. I have of late seen
some very learned men become in addition very
spiritual and prayerful men. And that makes me
pray that all our men of mind and learning may soon
become spiritual men and men of much prayer.

Let no one be admitted into this House unless she
is a woman of a sound understanding. For if she
is without mind she will neither know herself, nor
understand her teachers. For the most part they
that are defective in mind ever think that they
understand things better than their teachers. And
ignorance and self-conceit is a disease that is incur-
able ; and besides, it usually carries great malice along
with it. Many speak much and understand little.
Others, again, speak little and not very elegantly,
and yet they have a sound understanding. There is
such a thing as a holy simplicity that knows little
of anything but of how to treat with God. At the
same time commend me to holy people of good heads.
From silly devotees, may God deliver us ! While
all that is true, in the very act of prayer itself there
is little necessity for learning, for the mind then,
because of its nearness to the light, is itself im-

mediately illuminated. I myself, who am what I am, even I am a different person in prayer. It has often happened to me, who scarcely understand a word of what I read in Latin, when in deep prayer, to understand the Latin Psalms as if they were Spanish. At the same time, even for prayer, let those who have to teach and preach take full advantage of their learning, that they may help poor people of little learning, of whom I am one. Ministering with all learning and all intellectual ability to souls is a great thing, when it is done unto God. I have many experiences in prayer that I do not understand, and cannot explain or defend. Our Lord has not been pleased to give me the full intellectual understanding of all His dealings with me. That is the truth. Though you, my father, may think that I have a quick understanding, it is in reality not so. Sometimes my advisers used to be amazed at my ignorance how God carried on His work within me. It was there, but the way of it was a great deep to me. I could neither wade out unto God, nor down into myself. Though, as I have said, I loved to converse with men of mind as well as of heart. At the same time, my difficulties but increased my devotion, and the greater my difficulty the greater the increase of my devotion. Praise His Name.

ON PRAYER

(1) *The Price of Prayer.*—O Thou Lord of my soul, and my Eternal Good, why is it that when a soul resolves to follow Thee, and to do her best to forsake

all for Thee,—why is it that Thou dost not instantly
perfect Thy love and Thy peace within that soul?
But I have spoken unadvisedly and foolishly, for it is
we who are at fault in prayer, and never Thee. We
are so long and so slow in giving up our hearts to
Thee.   And then Thou wilt not permit our enjoy-
ment of Thee without our paying well for so precious
a possession.   There is nothing in all the world
wherewith to buy the shedding abroad of Thy love
in our heart, but our heart's love.   If, however, we
did what we could, not clinging with our hearts to
anything whatsoever in this world, but having our
treasure and our conversation in heaven, then this
blessedness would soon be ours, as all Thy saints
testify.   God never withholds Himself from him who
pays this price and who perseveres in seeking Him.
He will, little by little, and now and then, strengthen
and restore that soul, till at last it is victorious.   If he
who enters on this road only does violence enough to
himself, with the help of God, he will not only go to
heaven himself, but he will not go alone : he will
take others with him.   God will give him, as to a
good leader, those who will go after him.   Only, let
not any man of prayer ever expect to enjoy his whole
reward here.   He must remain a man of faith and
prayer to the end.   Let him resolve, then, that what-
ever his aridity and sense of indevotion may be, he
will never let himself sink utterly under his cross.
And the day will come when he will receive all his
petitions in one great answer, and all his wages in
one great reward.   For he serves a good Master, who
stands over him watching him.   And let him never

give over because of evil thoughts, even if they are
sprung upon him in the middle of his prayer, for the
devil so vexed the holy Jerome even in the wilderness.
But all these toils of soul have their sure reward, and
their just recompense set out for them.   And, I can
assure you, as one who knows what she is saying,
that one single drop of water out of God's living well
will both sustain you and reward you for another day
and another night of your life of life-long prayer.

(2) *Sin spoils Prayer.*—Now I saw that there would
be no answer to me till I had entire purity of con-
science, and no longer regarded any iniquity whatsoever in my heart.   I saw that there were some
secret affections still left in me, which, though they
were not very bad perhaps in themselves, yet in a
life of prayer such as I was attempting those re-
manent affections spoiled all.

(3) *Eighteen Years of Misery in Prayer.*—It is not
without very good reason that I have dwelt so long
on this part of my life.   It will give no one any
pleasure to see any one so base as I was.   And I
wish all who read this to have me in abhorrence.
I failed in all obedience, because I was not leaning
on my strong pillar of prayer.   I passed nearly
twenty years of my life on this stormy sea, constantly tossed with tempest and never coming
to harbour.   It was the most painful life that can
be imagined, because I had no sweetness in God,
and certainly no sweetness in sin.   I was often very
angry with myself on account of the many tears I

shed for my faults, when I could not but see how little improvement all my tears made in me. All my tears did not hold me back from sin when the opportunity returned. Till I came to look on my tears as little short of a delusion : and yet they were not. It was the goodness of the Lord to give me such compunction even when it was not as yet accompanied with complete reformation. But the whole root of my evil lay in my not thoroughly avoiding all occasions of sin, and in my confessors, who helped me at that time so little. If they had only told me what a dangerous road it was I was travelling in, and that I was bound to break off all occasions of sin, I do believe, without any doubt, that the matter would have been remedied at once. Nevertheless, I can trace distinctly the mercy of God to me in that all the time I had still the courage to pray. I say courage, because I know nothing in the whole world that requires greater courage than plotting treason against the King, knowing that He knows it, and yet continuing to frequent His presence in prayer. I spent more than eighteen years in that miserable attempt to reconcile God and my life of sin. The reason that I tell and repeat all this so often is that all who read what I write may understand how great is that grace God works in the soul when He gives it a disposition to pray on, even when it has not yet left off all sin. If that soul perseveres, in spite of sin, and temptation, and many relapses, our Lord will bring that soul at last—I am certain of it—to the harbour of salvation, to which He is surely bringing myself. I will say what I know by experience,—let him never cease from prayer, who has once begun to pray, be his life ever so bad. For prayer is the only way to amend his life, and without prayer it will never be mended. Let him not be tempted of the devil, as I was, to give up prayer on account of his unworthiness. Let him rather believe that if he will only still repent and pray, our Lord will still hear and answer. For myself, very often I was more occupied with the wish to see the end of the hour. I used actually to watch the sand-glass. And the sadness I sometimes felt on entering my oratory was so great, that it required all my courage to force myself in. In the end our Lord came to my help : and, then, when I had done this violence to myself, I found far greater peace and joy than when I prayed with regale and rapture. If our Lord then bore so long with me in all my wickedness, why should any one despair, however wicked he may be ? Let him have been ever so wicked up till now, he will not remain in his wickedness so many years as I did after receiving so many graces from our Lord. And this more I will say,—prayer was the true door by which our Lord distributed out all His grace so liberally to me. Prayer and trust. I used indeed to pray for help : but I see now that I committed all the time the fatal mistake of not putting my whole trust in His Majesty. I should have utterly and thoroughly distrusted and detested and suspected myself. I sought for help. I sometimes took great pains to get it. But I did not understand of how little use all that is unless we

root utterly all confidence out of ourselves, and place
it at once, and for ever, and absolutely in God. Those
were eighteen miserable years.

(4) *Aridity in Prayer.*—Let no one weary or lose
heart in prayer because of aridity. For the Hearer
of prayer comes in all such cases very late. But at
last He comes. And though He confessedly comes
late, He correspondingly makes up to the soul for all
His delays, and rewards her on the spot for all her
toil, and dryness, and discouragement of many years.
I have great pity on those who give way and lose all
this through not being taught to persevere in prayer.
It is a bad beginning, and very prejudicial to proficiency in prayer, to use it for the gust and consolation that a man receives at the time. I know by
my own experience, that he who determines to pray,
not much heeding either immediate comfort or dejec-
tion, he has got into one of the best secrets of prayer.
I am troubled to hear that grave men, and men of
learning and understanding, complain that God does not
give them sensible devotion. It proceeds from ignorance of the true life of prayer, and from not carrying
the cross into prayer as into all the rest of the spiritual
life. He who begins to pray should be well told that
he begins to plant a fine garden in very bad soil ; a
soil full of the most noxious and ineradicable weeds.
And that after good herbs and plants and flowers
have been sown, then he has to weed and water and
fence and watch that garden night and day and all his
life. Till the Lord of the garden is able to come and
recreate and regale Himself where once there was

nothing but weeds, and stones, and noxious vermin. Prayer, howsoever perfect in itself it may be, must always be directed in upon the performance of good works. We must not content ourselves with the gift of prayer, or with liberty and consolation and gust in prayer. We must come out from prayer the most rapturous and sweet only to do harder and ever harder works for God and our neighbour. Otherwise the prayer is not good, and the gusts are not from God. The growth and maturity and fruitfulness of the soul do not stand in liberty in prayer, but in love. And this love is got not by speaking much but by doing and suffering much. For my part, and I have been long at it, I desire no other gift of prayer but that which ends in every day making me a better and better woman. By its fruits your prayer will be known to yourselves and others.

At other times I find myself so arid that I am not able to form any distinct idea of God, nor can I put my soul into an attitude of prayer, though I am in the place of prayer, and though I feel that I know something of God. This mind of mine at such times is like a born fool or some idiot creature that nothing can bind down. I cannot command myself. I cannot properly say one *Credo*. At such times I laugh bitterly at myself, and see clearly my own natural misery. I come then to see the exceeding favour of the Lord in that He ever holds this insane fool fast in prayer and holiness. What would those who love and honour me think if they saw their friend in this dotage and distraction? I reflect at such times on the great hurt our original sin has done us. For it is from our first fall that all this has come to us that we so wander from God, and are so often utterly incapable of God. But it is not so much Adam's sin as my own that works in me all this alienation and inability and aridity. Methinks I love God ; but my actions, and the endless imperfections I see in myself, cause me great fear, and deep and inconsolable distress.

(5) *Prayer after Sin.*—Never let any one leave off prayer on any pretence : great sins committed, or any other pretence whatsoever. For by leaving off prayer the soul will be finally lost, while every return to prayer is new life and new strength, as I am continually telling you. I tell you again that the leaving off of prayer was the most devilish and the most deadly temptation I ever met with.

(6) *Meditation in Prayer.*—He who prays should often stop to think with whom he speaks : who he himself is who speaks : who Jesus Christ is through whom he speaks : what that country is to which he aspires : how he may best please Him who dwells there : and what he is to do so that his character and disposition may suit with God's disposition and character. Mental prayer, as I am wont to call it, is the constant meditation of such things as these. And mental prayer ought to be endeavoured after by all, though they have no virtues, because it is the beginning of them, and therefore the one interest of all men is at once to begin such prayer. But it will be exercised with no little difficulty unless

the steady acquisition of the virtues accompanies
it.　In prayer it is far best to be alone; as, for
our example and instruction, our Lord always was
when He prayed.　For we cannot talk both to
God and man at the same moment.　And, if we
feel too much alone, and must have company, no
company is comparable to Christ's company.　Let us
picture and represent Christ to ourselves and to His
Father as always at our side.　Those who pray with
proper preparation : that is, with much meditation on
the whole life and death of our Lord : on their own
death : on the last day, or such like, our Lord will
bring all such to the port of light.　Meditate much
on the Sacred Humanity of our Lord : what He
was on earth : what He said : what He did, and
what He suffered.　Because this life of ours is
long and uphill, which to pass well through needs
the constant presence with us of our great Exemplar,
Jesus Christ.

(7) *The Presence of God in Prayer.*—In prayer there
would sometimes come upon me such a sense of the
Presence of God that I seemed to be all engulfed in
God.　I think the learned call this mystical experience ; at any rate, it so suspends the ordinary
operations of the soul that she seems to be wholly
taken out of herself.　This tenderness, this sweetness, this regale is nothing else but the Presence of
God in the praying soul.　At the same time, I
believe that we can greatly help toward the obtaining
of God's Presence.　We obtain it by considering much
our own baseness, the neglect and the ingratitude

we show toward the Son of God, how much He
has done for us, His passion and terrible suffering,
His whole life so full of affliction, by delighting ourselves in His word and in His works, and such things
as these. And if in these reflections the soul be
seized with the Presence of God, then the whole soul
is regaled as I have described. The heart is filled
with relenting. Tears also abound. In this way
does the Divine Majesty repay us even here for any
little care we take to serve Him and to be with Him.
The life of prayer is just love to God and the custom
of being ever with Him.

(8) *Supernatural Prayer.*—In supernatural prayer
God places the soul in His immediate Presence, and
in an instant bestows Himself upon the soul in a way
she could never of herself attain to. He manifests
something of His greatness to the soul at such times:
something of His beauty, something of His special
and particular grace. And the soul enjoys God without dialectically understanding just how she so enjoys
Him. She burns with love without knowing what
she has done to deserve or to prepare herself for such
a rapture. It is the gift of God, and He gives His
gifts to whomsoever and whensoever He will. This,
my daughters, is perfect contemplation: this is
supernatural prayer. Now this is the difference
between natural and supernatural prayer: between
mental and transcendental prayer. In ordinary prayer
we more or less understand what we say and do.
We think of Him to whom we speak; we think
about ourselves and about our Surety and Mediator.

In all this, by God's help, we can do something, so to speak, of ourselves. But in pure supernatural and transcendental prayer, we do nothing at all. His Divine Majesty it is who does it all. He works in us at such elect seasons what far transcends and over-tops all the powers and resources even of the renewed nature. At the same time, as a far-off means of attaining to supernatural prayer, it is necessary to put upon ourselves the acquiring of the great virtues, and especially, humility : we must give up and resign ourselves wholly and entirely unto God. Whoever will not attempt to do this, with all the grace of God, that man will never come within sight of the highest prayer. Let him, in absolutely everything, seat him-self in the lowest place. Let him account himself utterly and hopelessly unworthy of everything he possesses, both in nature and in grace. Let him shun advancement. Let him apply himself to daily mortification, not of the body so much as of the mind and the heart, and let him be more than content with the least thing that God allows him, for this is true humility. In short, let His Majesty lead us in any way He pleases, and the chances are that He will soon lead us by these ways to a life of prayer and communion it had not entered into our hearts to conceive possible to such sinners as we are. Let no man be too much cast down, because he has not yet attained to supernatural prayer. God leads His people in the way that He chooses out as best for Him and for them. And he who stands low in his own eyes, may all the time stand high in God's eyes. Supernatural prayer is not necessary to salvation :

nor doth God require it of us. They shall not fail
of salvation who practise themselves in the solid
virtues. No, they may have more merit in His
eyes than their more favoured neighbours, because
their obedience, and their faith, and their love have
cost them more. Their Lord deals with them as
with strong and valiant men, appointing them travail
and trouble here, that they may fight for Him the
good fight of faith, and only come in for the prize
at the end. And, after all, what greater mark of a
high election can there be than to taste much of the
cross? Whom the Lord loveth, in that measure He
lays on them His cross. And the heaviest of all our
crosses is a life of sanctification and service without
sensible consolation.

(9) *Over-familiarity in Prayer.*—He was a man of
a powerful understanding. I thought on his great
gifts, and the possibilities there were in him of doing
great service if he were once entirely devoted to
God. He asked me to recommend him much to
God, and I did not need to be asked. I went away
to the place to which I used to retreat in cases like
this. And once there, I put myself into a state of
entire recollection, and began to treat with our Lord
in a way, when I think of it, of too great familiarity.
But it was love that spake, and every one allows love
great familiarity, and no one so much as our Lord.
My soul overlooked the distance between herself and
her Lord. She forgot herself, as she so often does,
and began to talk impertinences and to take too great
freedoms. I entreated our Lord with many tears.

I judged my friend to be already a good man, but I must have him much better, and I said so too freely, I fear. 'O Lord,' I remember I said, 'Thou must not deny me this favour that I ask. This is a man for us to make a friend of.' And far more than that. And He did it. Yes, He did it. O His immense bounty and goodness! He regards not the words but the affection with which the words are uttered. That must be so, when He endures with such an impertinent and over-familiar and irreverent wretch as I am; endures and answers. May He be blessed to all eternity!

(10) *The Best Result of Prayer.*—To Father Gratian. To-day I received three letters from your Reverence by the way of the head-post. The whole matter is in a nut-shell. That prayer is the most acceptable which leaves the best results. Results, I mean, in actions. That is true prayer. Not certain gusts of softness and feeling, and nothing more. For myself, I wish no other prayer but that which improves me in virtue. I would fain live more nearly as I pray. I count that to be a good prayer which leaves me more humble, even if it is still with great temptations, tribulations, and aridities. For it must never be thought that because a man has much suffering, therefore he cannot have prayed acceptably. His suffering is as incense set forth before God. Tell my daughters that they must work and suffer as well as pray, and that it is the best prayer that has with it the most work and the most suffering.

(11) *A Bishop taught to Pray.*—To Don Alonzo Velasquez, Bishop of Osma. Your Reverence enjoined me the other day to recommend you to God. I have done so: not regarding my own inconsiderableness, but your requisition and your rights. And I promise myself from your goodness that you will take in good part what I feel compelled to say to you, and will accept that which proceeds only from my obedience to you. Recognising, then, and representing to our Lord, the great favours He has done you in having bestowed upon you humility, charity, zeal for souls, and a strong desire to vindicate the Divine honour, I still besought the Lord for an increase in you of all these same virtues and perfections in order that you may prove as accomplished in all these things as the dignity of your office requires. Till it was discovered to me that you still wanted that which is the foundation of every virtue, and without which the whole superstructure dissolves, and falls in ruins. You want prayer. You want believing, persevering, courageous prayer. And the want of that prayer causes all that drought and disunion from which you say your soul suffers. That which was shown me as the way your lordship is henceforth to pray is this. You are to recollect and accuse yourself of all your sins since your last time of like prayer. You are to divest yourself of everything as if you were that moment to die. You are to begin by reciting to yourself and to God the Fifty-first Psalm. And after that you must say this. 'I come, O Lord, Bishop as I am, to Thy children's school of prayer and obedience. I come to Thee

not to teach, but to learn. I will speak to Thee, who am but dust and ashes.' And all the time set before the eyes of your soul Jesus Christ crucified, and ruminate on Him in some such way as this. Fix your eyes on that stupendous humility of His whereby He so annihilated Himself. Look on His head crowned with thorns. Fix your eyes on His nailed hands, His feet, and His side. Meditate on and interrogate every one of His wounds for you. It behoves you also to go to prayer with a most entire resignation and submission and pliantness to go that way in religion and in life that God points out to you. Sometimes He will teach you by turning His back on you: and, anon, by lifting up the light of His countenance upon you. Sometimes by shutting you out of His presence, and sometimes by bringing you into His banqueting-house. And you are to receive it all with the same equability of mind, knowing that He always acts for the best. Otherwise you will go to teach God in your prayers, which is not the proper scope and intent of prayer at all. And when you say that you are dust and ashes, you must observe and exhibit the proper quality of such. In our Lord's prayer in the garden, He requested that the bitterness and the terrible trial He felt in overcoming His human nature might be taken away. He did not ask that His pains might be taken away, but only the disgust wherewith He suffered them. And when it was answered Him that it was not expedient but that He should drink that cup, He had to master that weakness and pusillanimity of the flesh, as must all other men. One cannot be a great scholar, or even a finished courtier, without great pains and expense; and to be a scholar in the Church, and a minister, and a master in the science of Heaven, cannot be done without long time at school and much hard work.   And herewith I desist from saying more to your lordship, whose pardon I beg for all this presumption.   Which, however full it may be of defects and indiscretions, is not wanting in that zeal I owe to your service as one of the most wandering and gone astray of your lordship's flock. Our Lord preserve your lordship, and enrich you with the manifold increase of His grace.   I am, your lordship's unworthy servant and subject, Teresa of Jesus.

(12) *The proper Readers of what the Saint has Written.*—And now I return most humbly to beseech your Reverence, that, if you mean to impart to any one these things that you have made me write concerning prayer, let them be imparted to spiritual persons, and to persons of real insight only.   For, indeed, I have written for persons of exceptional experience and exceptional prudence only.   What I have written, I fear, very few are capable of.   But what am I, to speak thus about any but myself?   Farewell.—I am,

TERESA THE SINNER.

Twenty-first Thousand. Post 8vo, antique laid paper, cloth extra. Price 2s. 6d.

FIRST SERIES.

Bunyan Characters

LECTURES DELIVERED IN ST. GEORGE'S FREE CHURCH, EDINBURGH: BY ALEXANDER WHYTE, D.D.

CONTENTS

EDINBURGH AND LONDON :
OLIPHANT, ANDERSON AND FERRIER
AND ALL BOOKSELLERS.

*Tenth Thousand.   Post 8vo, antique laid paper, cloth
extra.   Price 2s. 6d.*

SECOND SERIES.

Bunyan Characters

LECTURES DELIVERED IN ST. GEORGE'S FREE CHURCH,
EDINBURGH : BY ALEXANDER WHYTE, D.D.

CONTENTS

EDINBURGH AND LONDON:
OLIPHANT, ANDERSON AND FERRIER
AND ALL BOOKSELLERS.

Post 8vo, antique laid paper, cloth extra.
Price 2s. 6d.

THIRD SERIES.

Bunyan Characters

LECTURES DELIVERED IN ST. GEORGE'S FREE CHURCH,
EDINBURGH : BY ALEXANDER WHYTE, D.D.

CONTENTS

EDINBURGH AND LONDON :
OLIPHANT, ANDERSON AND FERRIER
AND ALL BOOKSELLERS.

Sixth Thousand. Post 8vo, antique laid paper, cloth extra. Price 2s. 6d.

Samuel Rutherford

AND SOME OF HIS CORRESPONDENTS

LECTURES DELIVERED IN ST. GEORGE'S FREE CHURCH, EDINBURGH : BY ALEXANDER WHYTE, D.D.

CONTENTS

EDINBURGH AND LONDON :

OLIPHANT, ANDERSON AND FERRIER

AND ALL BOOKSELLERS.

Post 8vo, Art Linen, gilt top.   Price 3s. 6d.

Bible Characters
Adam to Achan
By ALEXANDER WHYTE, D.D.

CONTENTS

EDINBURGH AND LONDON:

OLIPHANT, ANDERSON AND FERRIER

AND ALL BOOKSELLERS.

www.ingramcontent.com/pod-product-compliance
Lightning Source LLC
Chambersburg PA
CBHW031443270326
41930CB00007B/839